50 THINGS KATE BUSH TAUGHT ME ABOUT THE MULTIVERSE

poems *Karyna*

50 THINGS TAUGHT ME MULTI

McGlynn

KATE BUSH ABOUT THE VERSE

SARABANDE BOOKS *Louisville, KY*

Publisher's Cataloging-In-Publication Data
(Prepared by The Donohue Group, Inc.)

Names: McGlynn, Karyna, author.
Title: 50 things Kate Bush taught me about the multiverse: poems / Karyna McGlynn.
Other Titles: Fifty things Kate Bush taught me about the multiverse
Description: Louisville, KY: Sarabande Books, 2022
Identifiers: ISBN 9781946448941 (paperback) | ISBN 9781946448958 (e-book)
Subjects: LCSH: Sex—Poetry. | Mental health—Poetry. | Climatic changes—Poetry.
Offenses against the person—Poetry. | Bush, Kate—Influence. | LCGFT: Poetry.
Classification: LCC PS3613.C486 A15 2022 (print) | LCC PS3613.C486 (e-book)
DDC 811/.6—dc23

Cover design by Danika Isdahl.
Cover art by Karyna McGlynn.
Interior design by Alban Fischer.
Printed in Canada.
This book is printed on acid-free paper.
Sarabande Books is a nonprofit literary organization.

This project is supported in part by an award from the National Endowment for the Arts.
The Kentucky Arts Council, the state arts agency, supports Sarabande Books with
state tax dollars and federal funding from the National Endowment for the Arts.

—for KT & all my teachers

CONTENTS

I just always thought of her as like the Phantom of the Opera . . . living in
this big castle with a piano that was ten times the size of a regular piano, just
playing the piano all day with sheer curtains blowing in the window . . .

—BIG BOI

We let the weirdness in
We let the weirdness in
We let the weirdness in
We let the weirdness in
We let the weirdness in

—KATE BUSH, "Leave It Open"

WAKING THE WITCH

A REAL ARTIST MAKES US FALL IN LOVE WITH GHOSTS

How could you leave me when I needed to possess you?
—KATE BUSH, "Wuthering Heights"

I want to haunt you into loving me. I need
the heavy lace hem of my nightgown to brush
your bare feet with fresh dew from the moors.
I want you to spend the rest of your life
hearing my song ripping through chimneys,
my mad footsteps pacing the attic above you,
my best dress: a plume of plasma descending
the stairs to a coronation that will never happen.

I'm running my icy fingers down the length of
the verso. I'm tapping lightly
on the paper that divides us.

If you hear it, I need you to know:
I have a way to cut a door
in the poem & step through it.
It's just this sheet that divides us.
It's just nothing.

I see you.
You can warm me.
Will you let me in.

IF YOU ASK PETER GABRIEL TO ASTRAL PROJECT

into your kitchen & hold you, he will.
Well, have you ever *tried* it?
Have you ever made a cocktail
for the hand that's haunting you?
Ever shaken your Intention into the Glass
& set it out on the Counter?
You have to be honest with the Universe.
You have to do right by your Audience.
They know when you're lying. Everyone
should get to embrace Someone
for at least seven seconds a day.
It's not much to ask.
It's not much to give. This safety's
the best kind of safety. Your gun's
growing cold & I like it. Let there
be sweetness. I will whittle the best
version of me & sail the kite of her
through your Saddest Bedroom Window.
Up before dawn? Follow me down
to the dark kitchen & I will
give you those seven seconds.
If you Show for Me,
I will Show for You.

THE GIRLS I GREW UP WITH WERE HARD

& inscrutable as mirrored cop glasses—
they reflected your fear right back at you.

They had shins like weapons & weren't afraid
to hurt you. They were gleaming, high-busted
& knew their way around a pool table.
They moved down the court of my adolescence:

Muscle & Hair & High-Five. They aced
precalculus & clattered down those awful halls
like the air of the high school was hugging them.

Their retainers glinted when they grinned
& when they laughed hard, you could sometimes
see the whole firmament of sparkly blue plastic.

They all took up Texas two-stepping—tan & top
heavy with God. They had cliques & Clinique
& intentions to study International Business.

Without intending to, their limbs sawed at the new
wood of me. I was soft & easily outdone.

I flung myself in the path of their collective
Jeep Cherokee & said my dad had stranded me.

They didn't stop—even though I smiled,
even though I said, *Please*. Even though

I'd baked them lemon cupcakes
& daubed Love's Baby Soft between my knees.

LOVE POEM WHEN WE RUN OUT OF CHICKENS

The way you love me: draining every
last drop of rat's blood into the goblet—
lest the crystal go to waste.
When you are sad you smell like moonshadow,
like ink in a sink. But when you look at me
like you *Like Me* it's like
someone set fire
to a field of goldenrod & let loose
a herd of wild game in my drawing room.

Your desire is cornflower blue
& slowly uncoiling my scarf.
It smacks the plate of crawfish
to confuse my scream. The whole affair
clatters to the floor! Even
the boiled ones scuttle.

The whole place is ablaze
but I wake up anyway
to the drip & the clink—
hair swept back in some rogue bow
of monstrous self-control.

I'm aware you might be a devil
but I'm a rut in your boulevard.

Maybe my Love-Bite is the price of pushing
your body cart up this Thunder Mountain.

Maybe it just rains all the time now
& rats no longer run from me.

I cradle my Old Faith like a New Baby
that refuses to open its eyes.

You & I have gifts to give out.
They're gathered in these skirts.
They're tucked like dark eggs
in the folds of the Sensual World.

It's true we are unlikely vampires—
twin foxes sucking the oxygen
directly from our Only Henhouse.

HALLOWEEN IN THE ANTHROPOCENE

& Memphis is out in Full Fang!
Skeletons skip down our pitted streets.
Whole families with matching hobo stipple
roam tragicomically through the sprawling
candy deserts: polka-dot bandanas
on sticks, flapping Chaplinesque shoes.

Unclaimed pumpkins pile high
behind razor wire. The air's thick
with caw & trouble. Our porch light's out
but we stay in, listening to the festive cackle
of semiautomatics in the autumn night.

Some faceless Handmaids do a spooky
hopscotch in a Walgreens parking lot.
Two drunk men in tiger masks loll from
the window of a passing truck to tell some
Handmaid she's "thicc as shit." Anyway,

Witches are back! They straddle plastic
brooms—streaming
across the moon's bright knuckle: hedge
witches & wicked witches. Waves
of Sabrinas: blonde bobs, black
headbands, whole hexes of freckles!
Here come the Elphabas & Endoras,
the Elviras & Elsas. Even a couple

of Baba Yagas—bewitched huts
strutting forth on sexy chicken legs!

So what if it's a bit
more *wink* than Wand.

We've stopped scaring ourselves
on purpose, stopped wearing our Weirds
on our Outsides. My sweetie's spilled on
the couch as Melted Clock. I park myself
on the dark stoop as Empty Pyrex Bowl.

According to the Post-it Note on my face,
my nickname is No-Treats-for-the-Wicked.
I'm a weird white lady on an unlit porch.
No one dare approach this childless abode—
not for phantom candy. Certainly
not for clarification.

APPLICATION TO MODEL
FOR HELMUT NEWTON

All I've ever really wanted to do
is stomp down Madison in nothing but
a full bush, a faux fur, a clutch
& a look of Horror.

I've shaken hands with some Hennessy
& held forth in an Oscar de la Renta.
I've been told my heels strike the sidewalk
like a pissed-off teacher
who already *told* you to Write in Silence.

I come with an attaché chained
to my wrist & a tennis bracelet
which makes a perceptible click
where its lips meet.

When I whistle for a taxi, two wolves
come running. My appetite for ennui
is enormous. Compare to my wasp waist.
Compare to this empty collins glass, this
sword skewering its cherry. Compare
to Crocodile Eating Ballerina.

It's true: I look sick in a suit.
My shadow: Vantablack at High Noon.
I prewarmed my thighs for you—

right on this terracotta balcony. I even
had the aesthetic sense to die
face-down in your pool. Dawn kisses
my temples with flame. Please
don't call this my Walk of Shame.

HOW TO DIE IN YOUR DREAMS

From behind a thicket of wine bottles
your partner tells the entire Italian restaurant
about your night terrors—how you wake up
shrieking, slicked with panic, fingernails
flecked with blood from the killer's face.

A silence. Then someone says,
"At least you don't *die* in your dreams."
But the truth is, you do die. This time,
you say so: how the dream grows grim
but won't spit you out—despite the Big Fall,
despite the knife in your neck.

(Your people poke at their manicotti.
The massacre of the antipasto platter.)

How sometimes they cut your tongue out first,
then throw it from a speeding van.
Your Confession on the asphalt behind you,
purple & pulsing like moose heart.

(Okay so maybe you're not great at small talk.)

Of course it's the other poet who asks:
"What happens in the dream *after* you die?"

That's the best part: it continues—
long after your input is required, long

after your matter matters at all.
Then there's a trapdoor. No choice
but Be Quiet. Just *listen* for once.

That might be the sound
of your teeth in the night
or one of your limbs in the grinder.

YOU MUST WAKE UP

else give up Ghosting. Your man
can't hear you. You are an empty wind
in his ear. The detective isn't picking up
any of the psychic snail trails
you're literally laying down.

Get thee to the forest!
Make a ball gown out of moss.
It's what you've always wanted.
With your body out of the way
the loam & animal musk might
breathe you back into being.

Follow the party of Artemis
to the center of things. Find
the deepest, blackest pool. The one
with a single moonbeam reaching
down through it, groping for a
dropped ring. Someone is singing
answers to questions you can't hear.

Music swims up the well
from another world.

The pool ripples its primordial silk.
It wants you slipped inside it.

You've always been good
at diving. When you were alive
& eleven, your mother drank
Jack Daniel's & tossed dimes
for you to fetch like a dog
in the deep end. Always *so good*

at finding the smallest, shiniest things
& thrusting them triumphantly
into the light, on the other side
of asphyxiation—smiling despite the fact
that nobody actually asked you
to bring them back.

WITCHES BE EVERYWHERE

& sometimes they'll be wearing botanical caftans
& giant amber rings
& other beautiful shit
& sometimes they'll walk right up to you
& start Singing
& they might even deem you Worthy
& then they might ask you to Dance
& you might like it a little Too Much
& sometimes they'll invite your ass over
& maybe make crepes
& sometimes they'll sweeten your tongue
               with Bénédictine
& make it *talk, talk, talk*
& if your talk is Real, you will gain Respect
& if your talk is Magic, you will gain a Realm
     but if there's no spark at the tip
         of your wand, fair warning—
              you may be tapped like overlong ash
       through that beautiful burn
    in the Big Flying Carpet!

A

CORAL

ROOM

I WAS BORN IN A CLOUD

with the rest of you.
Don't you remember?
I lived Down the Cloud
& was just as rare as you. We loved
to make love over British Columbia.
You loved to make it rain
over the Dark Fir Forest.
I flashed at you through the inky
limbs of the universe & you flashed back.
We were full of ourselves.
We simply brimmed.
Blurred our edges with Orgone,
switched boxes, got locked
in the libido broom closet. Took root
in the ruins of portable schoolrooms.
DNA was a constant scribble.
We dropped colorways into
the genetic Spirograph, watched them splash & chatter.
We untangled our yo-yos, said sorry
for our rude gesticulations.
We were weird sluts
in liquid gowns. So what?
The World (as we saw it) was Dry:
so we rained & we rained & we rained.

WE SING MOZART'S REQUIEM IN THE BACK OF THE CRUISER

You & I are seventeen & *oops*—
we've just shoplifted black boots
& Curve body spray from a box store.

We *were* going clubbing; now we're fleeing.
And it's raining. Two Men in Turtlenecks
rush from behind, tackle us to the dark
pavement, so we sing! We sing the Saddest

Songs we know: the stuff we learned for choir
the Year We Came in Third. We sing
to keep from crying. *Lacrimosa,* we wail. *Lacrimosa!*

The Turtlenecks parade us down the aisles
& shame us over the loudspeaker for the sake
of other late-night, dead-eyed shoppers
who might be likewise Tempted
to snatch a bright bauble—for shame!

A nauseating twist of agony in our harmony
now that we are Fallen. We worry hard
about Our Fathers. We Can't Believe It

when the cops handcuff us. We are *sure*
they're just scaring us. Even when they

stuff us in the back of the squad car, we
wait for somebody to produce the key.

As far as we understand, any Singer
who would express her remorse so Beautifully,
& so Publicly, must be Immediately Unbound.

"Straighten up, ladies," they are supposed to say,
cordially adjusting their heavy belts.

Instead, they take us Downtown. They
lower the radio chatter to listen as we thunder:
Dies Irae! Dies Illa! (Day of Wrath! Doom
Impending!) One officer softens, sorry for us.
The other looks nervous: "Hush, now."

We imagine Our Mothers: newly distraught
& accosting our closets. Side-by-Side
Close-Up as they discover our plunder!

Heaps of it. Plaid skirts & Mudd jeans.
Vanilla candles, crystal clutches, full-on
fairy wings, marabou fans, thigh-high
stockings balled into doll-sized silver
backpacks w/ bottles of Mini Thins,
gluey tubes of Great Lash, ironic kazoos,
Schlitterbahn shot glasses, or (shit!)
that black satin corset w/ shiny
hellfire flickering up its cinch!

And oh my god the stolen hoop skirts.
The light-up wands that play Magic Arpeggios
when waved at strangers. Those red stilettos
w/ little padlocks at the ankles!

Lord Have Mercy for Our Helpless Mothers
now quivering in the face of this Failure.
They sink to their knees in the Twin Spotlights
of our separate Klepto Heavens. *Kyrie eleison.*

Sweet Lord Jesus hear our plaint—
We sing of Day-Glo G-strings &
Lo! The lipsticks, lipsticks, lipsticks.

ONLY TWO THINGS WILL SAVE US NOW

Archery & Story Time.
If you must kill people, it must be
much harder for you to do it.
What is your experience
with fletching & kennings?
Do you call the muses down when you speak?
If not, what *are* you doing when you speak?
Have you been stretching?
Do you merely recite The Story
or do you Reanimate?
Oh, *no*—before you go,
you must be in our Tableau Vivant.
You will play the Hunted Doe—
trapped in the infinite amber
of our Drawn Breath,
of our Drawn Bow.

THIS WAS SUPPOSED TO BE AN ODE TO AQUA NET

To its chlorofluorocarbonic sexiness, like stilettos in a can.
To bangs like bandshells & the minor stardust
that glazed my dresser to a high sheen!

But something keeps showing up in the mirror
behind the poem & freaking me out:
that pack of Eighth-Grade Girls who pinned me
to the bathroom floor, sprayed Aqua Net
in my eyes & hissed, Say yr a dyke, *dyke* . . .

Say it . . . I didn't quite
say it. Instead, I cried
through lunch period,
through the rest of Texas
History, down the halls & straight
into the New Counselor's arms.

I rode the stallion of the New Counselor's
Concern into the sunset of the school day
& stepped out of the office with something
special: the Key to the Faculty Bathroom.

In third-period math, Candace saw me
staring & flashed a gun from under the hem
of her denim skirt. She gleeked smoothly
into my hair & said she would *hex* me.

"But why do they *hate* me?" I cried, nearly
fainting into the New Counselor's arms.

Surely, I knew. I spent my youth
yammering my way into undeserved glamour,
trying to distract from the fact that
I was unbearable. Meanwhile, the Faculty Bathroom
was dim & forgiving. The paper towels: softer.
The soap: pearly. There was even cinnamon
mouthwash & a little stack of Dixie cups.

But I was a snide, sneaky, preposterous girl
who used Big Words on purpose. I wrote
earnest poems about squirrels trying to stay
warm in winter & recited them in a Big Voice
& lapped up all the sweet glaze
of the Language Arts teachers' weird
love for me, like Robert Frost
had tapped my soul & sapped
my maple syrup Himself.

There I go again: snapping that big brass
Faculty Key to my backpack as if
I did something to deserve it.
See me clip-clopping down those
endless halls like a My Little Pony—
straight As tattooed across my ass!

YOU SEE, I'M ALL GROWN UP NOW

& easily wooed
into amusement
& wear Happiness
like a mauve gauze
over the too-small leotard of
my imposter syndrome
& I know how deep
the Forest Pool is—
& I know how haunted
& I know the names of the naiads
who run their tongues
down the lengths of this Solipsism
& I know some Humiliations
will never touch bottom

WHERE TO STASH YOUR WAX LIPS

Not the Live Oak, or stump of it.
Not the old Chevy in the back lot—
    chassis thrumming with yellow jackets.
Not the criminal fireplace, black-jawed,
    singe feathering the flocked wallpaper.
Not the coral davenport unsprung,
   or the monsters who must
swim deep in its florid coils.

Not where your aunt saw a specter—
   the shade of a Prim Lady rocking
    in her chair—but Up There,
the final flight of stairs, where
    your uncle lived & failed to live.
The steep flight, no light, the pitched
    ceiling, the single bed stillborn
on its iron frame—its mattress
    stripped & striped like nightshirts.

No, you must move this aside
    & grow low & pry the plywood
out like a rotted tooth. You must
   put your hand where you can't:
down the maw of the doll-sized
   crawl space. You must silt
your hand & feel for the shine:
   fleck your hand in the pink
    fiberglass field to know

the plump thing, the plaything—
                            & fetch it out.

You must put the piece in your mouth—
                         the soft cherry chew, the cartoon
you: Miss Coral Davenport! Find a floor-
                         length mirror & undrape. Loft
the drop cloth high, make the mum
                         pout speak: Come Hither, You.
Grotesque You. Eventually
                         You—you must chew on it.

I THOUGHT NO ONE WOULD EVER LOVE ME

so I lay in my daybed at night
& fashioned myself a Future
Wife. Someone like the girl
up the street with the old tan
Volvo. The one with one foot
in volleyball & the other
in drama club. Maybe I hid
her bleach. Maybe I gave
her pearls & a satin-trim
robe. Maybe I cut her
diploma into fleur-de-lis
& dipped them in the dark
chocolate of my chintzy
desires. I installed My Wife
in a woody, masculine den
& made her whippet-willed
& full of brandy. I stole her
hairspray & gave her a letter desk
instead & an actual inkwell.
I gave her lockable, leather-
bound love. I imagined her parents
somewhere safe, warm & out
of the way. We summered in Monaco,
read nothing but Daphne du Maurier,
took our sun at the Top of the City.
She had a smile like a high-wire act

& a signature like a sigil. I never
stopped loving the way she slid
into day-old stockings like a snake
reassuming its shed. In truth?
Her name was Jill. She wore
athletic shorts & never spoke
to me. So I renamed her Miriam
de Havilland & had her
handle my correspondence.
We cohabitated fantastically.
I installed paintings throughout
our Morning Room: storm-
flecked seas, gold-framed
& foaming at the mouth!

ON THE DUBIOUS HONOR
OF BEING PRETTIEST

Cry all you want, but don't ask questions.
Whatever you do, don't let go
of the polar bear's neck. Press your
breasts to his breath in the knowledge
you've made your father rich.
Bury your face in the bear's scruff.
Huff deeply. Maybe there's something
there after all. Now you must satisfy him.

Don't fall off. Stay away from his claws.
Stay away from his jaws.
When an anonymous man
visits your bed at night, make sure
to call the darkness around him
Nice Names. Learn to love
perpetual surrender. This is
what Pretty was built for.

Stay away from candles.
Steer clear of whispers & never
be alone with your mother. She will only
tempt you into sorrow. Consider this:

even if there's a Real Boy inside
the bear suit, do you really want to
unzip him? Oh no, now the bear's awake

& shaking you: Why couldn't you keep
your eyes closed? How does any of this
behoove you? What kind of Fool wants
out of the Castle in the first place?

NO CORROBORATING EVIDENCE

Keep Your Paws Off the Ice
of the Maritime Disaster Exhibit.
You might melt it. Then the tragedy
will repeat itself in miniature.
Keep your Hot Breath, please, off the Lifeboats.
Scratch your name off the place setting.
We *know* you, what you're willing to do:
stick a steak knife in the ice cream,
unleash an ice floe in the crab bisque.
Your table talk is uncouth.
Bedside manner: rude.
Are you willing to risk it?
You weren't on the guest list
in the first place. No one
will know how cold
the water was that night but you.
And we're sorry to say it, but
because you've continued to swim
you are an insufficient witness
to the foundering ship
of your own suffering.

IT'S SADDER IF YOU'RE A GIRL

so consider becoming one
before you die. Would it be
the worst thing? You could
defy expectations by being fast,
tall, sure of foot. You should
befriend a boy by making him king.
Stay away from the rope swing
as long as possible. Let someone see
you pray in private. Maybe memorize
all the poisonous plants. Stay out
of the woods, even if you're pretty
sure you know the way. Never go
when it's wet & windy—air rapt
with electricity! What do you *think*
happens when you wield your powers
alone & pit them against the weight
of a more compelling storyline?

Glitches, water sprites, your very womb:
a Whirlpool of Fate. Might as well turn
the hose on the whole endeavor.

It's sadder if
you're a strong swimmer,
a climber—child hexed
by Hubris, or kissed
by Hecate. The fallen tree

straddling the ravine
can fall again & damn that
rope is slick & brittle.

You know this.
You'll show them.

Where the branch creaks,
or current calls. When the wet rope
swings back for you, you'll catch
your death. Hear that
foghorn in the distance? God,
look at you: you're practically
trembling for it.

PULL OUT THE PIN

50 INCITING INCIDENTS

Unattended ketchup.
Komodo dragon teeth.
Someone stoked for summer camp.
Boys Collectively Shrugging.
Dry fingers on cheap felt.
The phrase "It's Not My Favorite."
Dusty horseback-riding trophies.
A freshly waxed sportscar.
A failed flip-flop. A "face-plant."
Braces caught in carpet fibers.
Trampoline with Exposed Springs.
A sneering thirteen-year-old.
The word "trigger" like a sting.
Bubbas, Bubble Yum, Body Horror.
The sun rising through an open
wound, a broken honeycomb.
Irregular Shapes on the Shelf.
A colleague who paints a wince in place
of a smile. Ice island in abandoned whiskey.
Teacher says, "I Probably Shouldn't Say This, But . . ."
The trigonometry of group dynamics.
That withering look, a slithering sound.
Someone saying, "Some fava beans
& a nice Chianti." A surreptitious selfie,
or friendship disguised as a Chamber
of Infinite Sadness. A Parade made
of Nothing but banners from local banks.
Special thanks to the charlatan mapmakers

who keep reinscribing the coastlines
of our reproductive freedoms. Here come
the Convenience Store Cakes! The itchy
fingers & complicated potluck signups.
Fever Dreams peppered with Fs.
Fears that flash like skunk stripes
when we pull back the pelt
of our Problems: PFAs, platitudes,
plastics, fascists, sadness, meat, mass
migration, messed-up algorithms,
broken sandals, bullet holes
in our PowerPoints, packs of hounds
sent to sniff us out & ensnare us
by our shifty Fox Feet. Where are we
supposed to hide our snowflakes when
the fire flails down the Hill & the tide
rises to meet its Hot Kiss? Why is this
armory so overstocked with weapons ill-
equipped for Mutual Survival?

SOMETIMES A GUY NAMED KEVIN LAUNCHES HIS RAFT IN YOUR RIVER

But he does it with vigor & you are too
lazy that day to spit him out.
Sometimes the sunrise paints its ice cream palette
right onto your cliff face & you are so
enamored with your own Apricot Majesty
you almost forget you have to share
the sight of yourself with a guy named Kevin.

You dip an oar in.
Kevin takes his waterproof speaker out.

Where birds once trilled & water thrilled
the wick of you, Kevin blasts
the thick twang of His Country
into Your Country.

HOW TO TALK THE MANIC AWAY

I used to be so mad—I had daggers coming out
my puffed sleeves. I decorated Easter baskets
with the plastic daisies of my Fury & mounted them
on Playtex-pink three-speeds. Every bike
I ever owned suffered a Spectacular Death:
hit by a gray Grand Am, tossed like a stone
into the quarry, snatched through a broken
window, found mangled in a ditch. I shook
my swampy sobs from their frames & ironed
my playbills for breakfast. I mounted my miscues
on the walls of a rocket. I covered my mistakes
in neon. I charged people to listen
to me scream. The people said my Hubris
would look better in the mouth
of a dinosaur. The people said I should marry
a disgraced news anchor. In a West Texas bar,
some girl asked if I'd seen the Marfa Lights.
I stood up whiskily on my stool & said,
"Bitch, I AM the Marfa Lights!"
I used to collect lace collars & white gloves
made for the nervous & the consumptive.
I stalked old ladies' estate sales.
Some still had boxes of seamed stockings
wrapped in tissue paper & lilac
toilet water & Bakelite hair combs.
None of this stuff ever fit or endeared me
to others. Imagine going through life
with white cotton seams around

your fingers. Imagine the whole world
saying, "Don't Touch." Still, in several
nightdresses I clambered over
a field of sods. There was a Desk
in the Distance with one light in its
Top Drawer. The night was open to me.
I took out my loudest shears
& cut a hole in the landscape
to make a space for the silence
I was immediately accused of violating.
My afterlife was a trial of ill-
fitting hats, spilled sugar & little girls
who loved their pet bunnies too much.
So much, they squeezed their lights out.
What shall I paint for the mourners?
An old schooner marooned in a field
of clover? A corpse that stinks its way
to the Truth? A bottle of warm
poppy milk? A dumbshow? Shall I
keep up appearances even though
I am slowly losing my sawdust
through an open seam?

GOLDEN AGE DRINKING

Our upstairs neighbor's apartment is leaking
"Moon River" again—it trickles
down the stairs & under our door.
It puts chopsticks in my chignon
& spritzes the place with Jean Patou.

The girl up there
has been crying
for three days straight.

She's pretty, pale & looks like
she's made of matchsticks, but
she heaves her Sadness around
the building like a Giant Toddler
on a short leash.

She never seems to sleep.
When she checks her mailbox
we can see she's a cutter.

This is the late '90s though,
so what's happening
feels more like an Aesthetic
than a Situation.

In the Mansion of Many Apartments,
we keep facing a choice:
whether to leave certainty

for something else
which might be messy,
awkward, or mean.

When I try to look through
the prism of my early twenties
all I really see is gin, scorn
& a marble chess set. My stupid
Scorpio Earrings. I took baths,
felt wrath. I didn't even have
a real job, just a Lover who fed me
slivers of cheese & apple off a knife
in a silver hammock we scored
for free on Craigslist. Did I think I was
some kind of French Duke or what?

By day I did my vocal exercises & listened
to cassette tapes: etymological lectures, French
lessons, Robert Lowell intoning "nine-knot yawl"
& "I myself am hell; nobody's here—"

By night I blew long curls of lavender
smoke & Julie London tunes through
the cracks in our ceiling like I was
fumigating millennial centipedes.

Our upstairs neighbor?
The short answer is
I don't know what happened.

None of us did
a damn thing but drink & egg each
other on with increasingly melancholic music.

In hallways, I still see her
rhinestone spine flash & wriggle back
into the shadow of the fact:
we made a Whole Skit of her
but never even knocked.

FUN FACTORY

Time packs my Play-Doh
back in the trunk of his Fun Factory.
The bright clench of our first
apartment: old grease & rose spritz.
The tight asterisk of His Rule
exerting its squeeze. As if love
were a matter of pure muscle:
Man vs. His Best Packing Skills.

I used to dream an invisible giant
had a fetish for my flesh,
would steal it off my sleeping body—
abscond with my skin
in a too-small suitcase.

Later in the lair,
he would unroll my skin
in front of a floor-length mirror—
hold it up to his form
like a mail order teddy—his eyes
looking straight through my
eyeholes & back into a better
version of himself.

Then he climbed inside my skin.
Evicted everything that was Not Him.
My energy squeezed out the pale

lace & disbanded. That was the end
of my story. I saw it all happen.

The giant continued
to live in the drag of me. Nobody noticed.
Even when he told the truth about what he'd done.
Even when he wrote it down.

I STAND OUTSIDE THIS WOMAN'S WORK

& watch Kevin Bacon conjure fake tears in a Real Hallway
& I am Real Tears in a fake hallway
& "Procreation is *gross* though"

I'm nine & a half, watching "The Miracle
of Life" on my mother's bed

Stirring my shells & cheese
I see that Big '70s Bush split in twain!
I drop my spoon
Surely, I am not this Bloody Meat

I march down to the kitchen
& make an announcement:
"I am *never* having a baby!"

My mother takes me to a Sunday
matinee of *She's Having a Baby*

In the dark, we share a giant pickle
in wax paper & weep openly
for Poor Kevin Bacon

There's been a complication with the birth
            & Kate Bush croons
        "Ooh, it's hard on the man, now his part is over . . ."

In line to buy the soundtrack at Sam Goody
    my mother tells me a secret—
        "Women who don't give birth
            tend to get cancer."

    Everything begins to split:

Maybe the mother's body   splayed on the table
or the pregnant calico   unseamed by coyotes
or the way I learn my left   splits before my right
how sometimes at night   my dead dance
teacher hovers over my bed   with a black magic
marker & keeps score   on my headboard
Suck it in, suck it up   she hisses & squints

    I get addicted to split-   screen sex comedies
    starring impossible people   from the '60s
    leading Double Lives   in Twin Beds

Every adult I know is in a trial   separation
& none of them   seem to be
whispering double   entendres into a Princess phone

    Meanwhile, under the microscope
        pond scum cells *shimmer*
            & for god's sake *mitose*

Something wicked falls
    sideways from my mouth   "Why don't you have
            your *own* grandkids then?"

This is more or less what my mother does
    but not without complications—

What an awkward sort of sadness   to wait out in the hallway

                                            with Poor Kevin Bacon

while Birth & Death sing their biggest hits

                                            without you

I WAKE UP IN THE UNDERWORLD OF MY OWN DIRTY PURSE

My stage name is Persephone.
I perform nightly for a smattering
of ill-informed Tic Tacs.

Now that I'm finally tiny,
I only have two fears:
that someone will leave
my Whole World in the sun
unattended & gravity's strap
might one day strain & break.

Down here, no one desires me,
but there are relatively few decisions:
what flavor gum to huff,
how many grains of granola.

I spend my time rolling around
with lipsticks: matte nudes
& cabernet mistakes that looked
better on the models. I bind
my thighs with dental floss,
finally learn the aerial arts.

There are bobby pins.
I have to watch myself. I become

begummed, magnetized.
Things stick. Sometimes I can't
shake them. For a whole week
I was Working Shit Out
with a broken necklace that had me
ensnared by the hair.

In my dark bordello,
Bic lighters are barges
out in deep water. I taste
the tang of their flint sharpening,
receding, hear the cargo
sloshing, the boatswain's call
at the far edge of my sanity.
Sometimes keys wash up to me—
all faint numbers & silver teeth.
I no longer know what they open.

More than once, I've considered
setting the place on fire.
So easy. Plenty to kindle:
petrified pretzel logs, illegible receipts,
& sometimes, incredibly, a tampon
escaped from its casing—string
like a fuse on a soft stick of dynamite.

On hot nights, I unscrew my purse
perfume & move my naked body
like a question across the cool
roller-ball. She is a Silent Oracle
who only answers in spirits
& fumes: pomegranate, lily
of the valley, amber, wet fern,

African violet. I have eternity
to translate this Olfactory Code
into a working escape plan.

For lack of space: Please Help.
This is what I've been reduced to.
I hope someone Up There is looking
for me. I hope my Mother is
burning the goddamn crops.

HOW TO STOP RAPING THE MUSE

When I was twenty-two, my poetry professor
leaned back in his Naugahyde chair & told me
he wanted me to write Like a Woman.

I took this to mean he wanted my poems
to swaddle him in their tight little couplets.

He would have *hated* that line.

He was dramatically disappointed
when I couldn't identify the names
of the trees in the quad. "You're like a child,"
he said. "You profess to be a poet, but you don't
even know the names of the things
around you & if I were a Girl Poet I would make it
my business to know the difference
between a Willow & a Cypress."

Next semester, the professor said,
"Okay, Miss Witty, where's the vulnerability?"
Then someone in workshop suggested
my poems had Teeth but no Tenderness,
then everybody snapped in assent.

In the Spring, my lines were called
Sharks & Shameless
Hussies. Someone said

my similes were made of Raw Meat.
I was Slutty with Commas. My speakers were all
Smack Talk & No Smiles.

The professor summoned me
to his office, said he needed
my poems to feel more pregnant—
that the forest of my poetry was impenetrable,
that I needed to leave a trail of milk & candy
if I wanted anybody to follow me into the woods.

I took these suggestions
in the best possible way.

The next professor brought in a Guest Poet
(his buddy from grad school)
whose Three (3) Main Suggestions were:
Don't Flirt with Greatness,
Make Speaker Softer . . . Less Shrill,
& Stop Raping the Muse.

Finally, my dissertation director
looked at me over the fishbowl margaritas
of my penultimate semester—
waving mosquitoes away with my manuscript—
& said, "Why don't you get married
& have a couple of babies? For many of us
happiness isn't an option, but it is for you."

When he died, I avoided my phone,
walked around in a fugue state for three days.

He would have approved
of that kind of ending
but never whatever
this is.

WOW

COME UP & BE A KITE

Bring out your Best Spangles
       & your Blackest Blacks
          & your Wettest Plums
             & your Pumas on Leashes.

Put on your Sparkle Bones
       & your Murder Eyes—don't
          spill your Blueblood Soda
             all over the Davenport!

What are you doing Down There
       in Adult Detention, when you need
          to work on your Backbend
             & your Book Drag?

"At eye level, it isn't Good Enough"
       & you only need One Hand
          to hoist your Bones Up,
             to let your String Go—

TIFFANY CONDITIONER

"My name is Tiffany Conditioner,"
I told my mother one day. "Tiffany,"
I told the mailman, *Conditioner*,"
shaking his hand. Everyone was always
"disappointed" but kind of faking it
because I saw them laughing.

I brought down the stepladder so I could
reach my adolescence faster. I bought
a dress that made me look like a statuette
but nobody wanted to win me.

Even though I brushed my hair
100 strokes before bed & made everyone
stuffed rabbits for Easter. Everyone said
I was weird & wanted to kiss them.

So I wore a lamé stole & shone inside
its bright lie. I slumped across
the flimsy sets of Seventh-Grade Drama
like a malingering child movie star
forced to smoke. My teacher said I didn't
understand the difference between glamour
& humor, so I went to the chalkboard
& powdered my face with erasers.

I sold more Poinsettias than Anyone!
I still don't understand why that doesn't count.
I packed my navel in a crate & gave it
to charity so I wouldn't stare at it.
Still, everyone was So Disappointed.

IF YOUR GLAMOUR IS REAL

you shimmer
through your plainness
& sprinkle extra star-dew on the Thirsty
& if your glamour is real, you bring
your own lamplight
& everything you say sharks
through the room
& people part like seagrass
& babies stare big-eyed
like you are a bad sprite
sprayed with good sequins
& sent down the produce aisle
by a Higher Power
to anoint them in the peaches!
& if your glamour is real, you, too
will be anointed in the peaches!
& you can wear bigger hats than mere mortals
& you can be On the Level
& you can Level Up
& you can float Above the Level
& you can sip the Level's bathwater up
with a Big Stripey Straw!
& when you ask, "Is this the juice
that keeps me so Fresh?"
the cosmos blinks once for *Yes*

WHITE DRESS VS. RED DRESS

If the White Dress
is a Catholic Prom

     the Red Dress
     is a Medieval Abattoir—

& if the White Dress
is a Haunted Hospital   the Red Dress
     is a Heart O' the Hour—

Where White Dress twins & triples   Red Dress remains
     the Only Child

While White Dress wings & gurneys   Red regurgitates
     the *Urgency*

   I guess

     you're supposed to want
     the Red Dress
     the corset & orchid
     the *No* disguised as *Yes*

   Surely something about this
   dress discrepancy must explain
   why some people just can't dance
   on the same team; what does it mean

     to prefer a Misty Moor
to a Fog Machine?

Or a Tracer Effect to a Human Hand?

Some people only love Mystery
in Day Makeup—

Others vamp with the Void
& name it Stage Directions

Meanwhile White Dress has dreadful potential: it could become

Red in a Second—

just a flick of the wrist
just a tip of the bucket

50 OTHER WORDS FOR SNOW

Chalk Drop

Blancmange   Crunch Time

Long-Necked Swan   Lambskin Scrim

Sparkletongue
Shaven Angel

Ectoblast   Twirly-Fur   Zest of Skibunny

B-r-r Church
"Concupiscent Curds"
Rowhouse Blow

Bisquick Sift   Asgard's Wrath   Eraser Spank

Shivered Fox
Middle Distance
Forlorn Bjorn

Edwardian Ash   Dendrite Flight   Neverwarm

Xylographer's Relief
Bundlefluffen
Wonkavision

Cream of Opal   Cape of Jadis   Smoker's Bane

Quivering Whippet   Quark Swarm

Flusterslush

Veritas
Kicker's Freeskate

Powderwig's Wish   Lost Mare   Wallace Stevens
Ulaanbaatar
                    Woodman's Whistle
                                        Fill-in-the-Blank
                Yarmulke Dust
                Hufflepuff
                Great British Baking Powder

Rough & Tumble   Haunt O' the Owl   Redacted World

        Veni Vidi Vici   Venus in Furs

                Glitter-Ghosted
                Writer's Block
                "Zero at the Bone"

IF YOU KEEP HITTING THOSE HIGH NOTES

strangers will stop asking you
to prove you're a woman.
Real Women remember birthdays.
Real Women have bosoms
that feed whole villages.
Real Women thrust
their hips when angry
& make their lips both big & small.

You confuse us.
You say you are Not Angry
yet we've seen you enjoy the footage:
prey trouncing predator!

In terms of Taking Them Down: you must do it
with an impossible note—one that explodes
into blossom when it touches them.
Their hearts must stand up, beet-red & lacy.
You need them to lower their fear sticks & listen.
You need them to curate this Exhibition of Love.

NATURE IS SO MELODRAMATIC, ALWAYS

haunting the bushes & succumbing
to the blaze & choke of its own
Coppery Cotillion Gown
before springing back to life
in Season Two.

How long can it last? This bottle
of ichor, this cyclical self
softly locked & unlocking, this
rabbit-fur chastity belt.

What swells in us, stressing its pink
past perfect? We must knock
on a New Door. How about this one:
square, bone-handled, barely
aware of our Animal Being.

Deep in the keyhole, something winks.
Night raises her Cold Cathedral.
We step through the portal together,
a single seed between us.

IF OUR ART MUST OUTLIVE US

we must understand what that means
& stop entwining our genes—
to need to, but not to.

In place of I Love You
a thick pine knot—our pressed bodies
bleeding bottomless tar into time's pit.

Some of our desires must be
wrapped in blue tea towels
& left in the reeds to die.

I wonder how many demons
we've strummed up with
the careless grammar of Bad Fantasy.

Anyway, we all have to change
now that Hate's blasted holes
in the hull of our starship.

Hush. This doesn't have to be
the opposite of happiness. Our rudder
is not married to this riverbed.

"I put this moment here"

NOTES

The Big Boi quote on the epigraph page is from an August 22, 2018, *Pitchfork* "VERSES" episode in which he discusses Kate Bush's musical influence—and memorably imitates the sound of the Fairlight synthesizer in "Running Up That Hill (A Deal With God)" from Bush's album *Hounds of Love* (1985).

The Kate Bush quote on the epigraph page is a lyric from the song "Leave It Open," which appears on her album *The Dreaming* (1982).

All the sections in the book are titled after Kate Bush songs. "Waking the Witch" is the title of a song on the second side of *Hounds of Love* (a.k.a. *The Ninth Wave*, Bush's conceptual suite about a woman floating alone in the water at night). "A Coral Room" is the title of a song from Bush's album *Aerial* (2005). "Pull Out the Pin" is the title of a song from her album *The Dreaming*. "Wow" is the title of a song from her album *Lionheart* (1978).

"A Real Artist Makes Us Fall in Love with Ghosts"

The epigraph "How could you leave me when I needed to possess you?" is a lyric from Kate Bush's 1978 debut, "Wuthering Heights." The song was inspired by a 1967 BBC film adaptation of Emily Brontë's 1847 gothic novel *Wuthering Heights*. (Fun fact: Brontë and Bush are both Leo babies born on July 30!) My lines "It's just this sheet that divides us. / It's just nothing" deliberately echo Arnold Friend's dialogue ("It's just a screen door. It's just nothing") in Joyce Carol Oates's terrifying 1966 short story "Where Are You Going, Where Have You Been?"

Other echoes include John Keats's poem fragment "This living hand, now warm and capable," the 1847 Charlotte Brontë novel *Jane Eyre*, the film *Let the Right One In* (2008), and the film *Poltergeist* (1982).

"If You Ask Peter Gabriel to Astral Project"

The last two lines of this poem are from Peter Gabriel's "Sledgehammer" (*So*; 1986): "Show for me, I will show for you." I also had in mind the moving music video for Peter Gabriel and Kate Bush's duet "Don't Give Up" (1986), which features Gabriel & Bush embracing each other while singing the whole song.

"Love Poem When We Run Out of Chickens"

This poem is partially inspired by the movie *Interview with the Vampire* (1994). I also include a wink to Kate Bush's 1989 single "The Sensual World."

"Halloween in the Anthropocene"

I borrow the term "Chaplinesque" from Hart Crane's 1933 poem of that name. "Handmaids" refers to costumes inspired by the 2017 Hulu adaption of Margaret Atwood's 1985 novel, *The Handmaid's Tale*. "Sabrinas" refers to costumes inspired by the Archie Comics character Sabrina Spellman (especially as stylized in the 2018 Netflix adaptation of *The Chilling Adventures of Sabrina*). "Elphabas" refers to costumes inspired by Gregory Maguire's character Elphaba Thropp in the 1995 novel *Wicked: The Life and Times of the Wicked Witch of the West* (especially as popularized by Idina Menzel's performance in the 2003 Broadway musical *Wicked*). "Endoras" refers to costumes inspired by Agnes Moorehead's character on the classic TV sitcom *Bewitched*. "Elviras" refers to costumes inspired by Cassandra Peterson's TV portrayal of the character Elvira, Mistress of the Dark. "Baba Yagas" refers to costumes inspired by interpretations of the Slavic folklore figure. "Melted Clock" alludes to Salvador Dalí's 1931 painting *The Persistence of Memory*.

"Application to Model for Helmut Newton"

This poem was inspired by Helmut Newton's photography. I allude to several images in the collection *White Women* (Stonehill, 1976). *Crocodile Eating Ballerina* is the title of a Newton photo of a scene from the 1983 Pina Bausch ballet performance, *Die Keuschhleitslegende* ("The Legend of Virginity").

"You Must Wake Up"

"You must wake up" is a spoken lyric from the opening montage of voices in the 1985 Kate Bush song "Waking the Witch." The song dramatizes a witch trial.

"Witches Be Everywhere"

   The title refers to something I overheard one girl say to another in the restroom at a David Bowie tribute concert. My line "& make it *talk, talk, talk*" echoes Sylvia Plath's 1963 poem "The Applicant."

"I Was Born in a Cloud"

   "I was born in a cloud" is the opening lyric of Kate Bush's song "Snowflake" on her album *50 Words for Snow* (2011). My lines "Blurred our edges with Orgone, / switched boxes, got locked / in the libido broom closet" allude to the theories of the psychoanalyst Wilhelm Reich. Kate Bush's 1985 song "Cloudbusting" (*Hounds of Love*) tells the story of Wilhelm Reich's cloudbuster device through the eyes of his son Peter Reich.

"We Sing Mozart's Requiem in the Back of the Cruiser"

   The lines in Latin are lyrics from Mozart's Requiem in D Minor. "Schlitterbahn" refers to a popular water park in New Braunfels, Texas.

"You See, I'm All Grown Up Now"

   The title is taken is the opening lyric of Kate Bush's song "The Fog" on the album *The Sensual World* (1989).

"I Thought No One Would Ever Love Me"

   The poem includes a reference to the Kate Bush song "Top of the City" from her album *The Red Shoes* (1993). The poem is also inspired by Daphne du Maurier's 1938 gothic novel *Rebecca*, Helmut Newton's photography, and Robert Browning's 1842 dramatic monologue "My Last Duchess."

"On the Dubious Honor of Being Prettiest"

   This piece is partially inspired by the Norwegian fairy tale "East of the Sun and West of the Moon."

"It's Sadder If You're a Girl"

   This piece is partially inspired by Katherine Paterson's book *Bridge to Terabithia* (1977).

"Sometimes a Guy Named Kevin Launches His Raft in Your River"

Apologies to all the Kevins! I know many lovely Kevins and this poem is not based on any of them. The choice was purely a sonic one. Plus, I've always been low-key envious of the Lionel Shriver title *We Need to Talk About Kevin* (Counterpoint, 2003).

"How to Talk the Manic Away"

The "Marfa Lights" refers to an unidentified aerial phenomenon outside of Marfa, Texas. I've witnessed these mystery lights on two occasions and they defy explanation. This poem was also inspired by the movie *Alice* (1988).

"Golden Age Drinking"

"Moon River" refers here to the Henry Mancini and Johnny Mercer song as originally performed by Audrey Hepburn in the 1961 movie *Breakfast at Tiffany's*. The "Mansion of Many Apartments" alludes to an extended metaphor in an 1818 letter written by John Keats to John Hamilton Reynolds. My "French Duke" bit borrows its premise from a scene in *The Mighty Boosh* episode "Killeroo" (2004) where Howard Moon says to Vince Noir, "You? You're a French duke if I ever saw one. You lay around on hammocks all day eating soft cheese." The speaker quotes a recording of Robert Lowell reading his poem "Skunk Hour" from *Life Studies* (Farrar, Straus & Giroux, 1959) in the following lines: "Robert Lowell intoning 'nine-knot yawl' / & 'I myself am hell; nobody's here—.' Lowell's speaker echoes Satan's speech in Milton's *Paradise Lost*: "Which way I fly is Hell; myself am Hell" (Book 4, line 75). "Julie London tunes" refers to songs on Julie London's album *About the Blues* (1957).

"Fun Factory"

The title refers to the classic Play-Doh toy.

"I Stand Outside This Woman's Work"

"I stand outside this woman's work" is a lyric from Kate Bush's song "This Woman's Work," which was originally featured in the film *She's Having a Baby* (1988), starring Elizabeth McGovern and Kevin Bacon. The song later appeared on Kate Bush's album *The Sensual World*. "The Miracle of Life" refers to a 1983 episode of *NOVA* which concludes with footage of a woman giving birth.

"I Wake Up in the Underworld of My Own Dirty Purse"

The poem makes several allusions to the mythological figures Persephone and Demeter—particularly as they relate to the Eleusinian Mysteries.

"How to Stop Raping the Muse"

The title refers to a piece of "advice" I received from a poet-in-residence when I was an undergraduate. The poem dramatizes a composite of writing workshops and professors I've worked with over the years.

"Come Up & Be a Kite"

"Come up and be a kite" is the opening lyric of the Kate Bush song "Kite" from her album *The Kick Inside* (1978). The line "At eye level, it isn't Good Enough" is taken from the same song. The capitalization of "Good Enough" is my own stylization of Bush's vocal treatment. Some of the imagery in this poem is inspired by the album cover art of Roxy Music's *For Your Pleasure* (1973), which features Amanda Lear holding a black panther on a leash. (I do not condone using animals as fashion props.)

"White Dress vs. Red Dress"

This poem was inspired by the classic debate among Kate Bush fans about which version of the music video for "Wuthering Heights" is better: the one where Kate dances in an iconic white dress, or the one where she dances in an (even more) iconic red dress. Both versions are pioneers in early music video innovation, and both are captivating examples of Lindsay Kemp's influence on Kate's style of choreography and storytelling.

I also allude to the climactic scene of Stephen King's 1974 novel *Carrie*— especially as imagined through Brian de Palma's lens in his 1976 film adaptation starring Sissy Spacek.

"50 Other Words for Snow"

This poem is an homage to the titular track on the Kate Bush album *50 Words for Snow*. In Bush's song, Stephen Fry recites all 50 "words for snow" as Kate ecstatically counts him down. The poem contains many allusions and a few direct quotations. "Blancmange" refers both to the English New Wave band and to the white, gelatinous dessert. "Concupiscent Curds" is a stylized allusion to the 1922 Wallace Stevens poem "The Emperor of Ice-Cream." "Wonkavision" refers here to the 1971 movie *Willy Wonka and the Chocolate Factory*, based on Roald Dahl's 1964 children's novel *Charlie and the Chocolate Factory*. My phrase "Cape of Jadis" refers to Jadis the White Witch, a character from C. S. Lewis's The Chronicles of Narnia series. The Latin word "Veritas" refers here to the Roman goddess of truth. "Hufflepuff" refers to one of the four Hogwarts houses in the Wizarding World universe. "Veni, vidi, vici" ("I came; I saw; I conquered") is popularly attributed to Julius Caesar. *Venus in Furs* is the title of an 1870 novella by Leopold von Sacher-Masoch, which later inspired the 1967 Velvet Underground song of the same name. It's also the name of the fictional glam rock band that backs Brian Slade ("Maxwell Demon") in the classic 1998 Todd Haynes film *Velvet Goldmine* (one of my all-time favorites—a visual feast!—and truly a *must* for music lovers). The phrase "Zero at the Bone" is from the 1865 Emily Dickinson poem "[a narrow Fellow in the Grass]" (Franklin 1096).

"I put this moment here" is a lyric from Kate Bush's song "Jig of Life" on *Hounds of Love*.

ACKNOWLEDGMENTS

Kind thanks to the editors and interns of the following magazines where earlier versions of many of the poems in this collection first appeared:

32 Poems, *Arts & Letters*, the *Best American Poetry* blog, *Grist*, *Handcastle Magazine*, *Matter*, *Mississippi Review*, *New England Review*, *The Pinch*, *Poet Lore*, *RealPoetik*, *Southern Indiana Review*, *Stirring*, and *Tupelo Quarterly*.

"I Stand Outside This Woman's Work" and "I Wake Up in the Underworld of My Own Dirty Purse" were awarded the 2020 Rumi Prize for Poetry from *Arts & Letters*.

Thank you to Bruce, who once burned a *Hounds of Love* CD, then slipped it under my front door in the night like some kind of magical Kate Bush postman. And to the person who texted me one cold winter's night in 2008 to invite me to a party where the password was "Kate Bush." And to that group of Obies wildly singing "Wuthering Heights" in the kitchen of the co-op as I ate tofu off a Frisbee in, like, 2016. You unintentionally inspired this book!

A big thank you to my colleagues at CBU, particularly those in the Rosa Deal School of Arts, for their deep kindness and unwavering support. And to my hilarious, brilliant students who help make me a better teacher and a braver writer.

I am indebted to many writer pals who generously lent their time and brilliance—especially Alice Bolin, Josh Urban Davis, Dan Hornsby, Josh Kalscheur, Cate Marvin, Kathryn Nuernberger, Emily Skaja, Ed Skoog, Analicia Sotelo, Leigh Stein, Adam Theriault, Marcus Wicker, and Caki Wilkinson.

My deepest gratitude to the talented and passionate crew at Sarabande Books—particularly Sarah Gorham, Danika Isdahl, Kristen Renee Miller, and Joanna

Englert—for bringing this project (our third book baby!) to life. I'm also very grateful to Emma Aprile for her keen eye.

To my fiancé, Brent Nobles, who loves Kate Bush just as much as I do, and who brought his magic at every stage.

Finally, to Fruit, my familiar. And to Kate, who got me through it. "All the love."